Parrots

ABDO
Publishing Company

A Buddy Book
by
Julie Murray

VISIT US AT
www.abdopub.com

Published by Buddy Books, an imprint of ABDO Publishing Company, 4940 Viking Drive, Suite 622, Edina, Minnesota 55435. Copyright © 2002 by Abdo Consulting Group, Inc. International copyrights reserved in all countries. No part of this book may be reproduced in any form without written permission from the publisher.

Printed in the United States.

Edited by: Christy DeVillier
Contributing Editors: Matt Ray, Michael P. Goecke
Graphic Design: Maria Hosley
Image Research: Deborah Coldiron
Cover Photograph: Digital Vision Ltd.
Interior Photographs: Eyewire Inc., Minden Pictures, Photodisc

Library of Congress Cataloging-in-Publication Data

Murray, Julie, 1969-
   Parrots/Julie Murray.
      p. cm. — (Animal kingdom)
   Summary: Describes the physical characteristics, behavior, and habitat of parrots and discusses specific species such as the African gray parrot, macaw, and kakapo.
   ISBN 1-57765-705-5
     1. Parrots—Juvenile literature. [1. Parrots.] I. Title. II. Animal kingdom (Edina, Minn.)

QL696.P7 M88 2002
598.7'1—dc21

                     2001053723

Contents

Parrots .4

What They Look Like 6

Climbing Birds 8

Eating And Nesting 10

African Gray Parrots 12

Macaws 14

Kakapos 16

Parrot Chicks 18

Parrots At Risk 20

Important Words 22

Web Sites 23

Index 24

Parrots

There are more than 300 species, or kinds, of parrots. Parakeets, macaws, cockatoos, and lovebirds are all parrots. Wild parrots live in South America, Central America, Africa, Australia, and Asia. The parrot's habitat is commonly warm, wet, and full of trees.

Many people have pet parrots.

People enjoy having parrots as pets. People like hearing parrots mimic sounds. Some parrots are good at mimicking what people say. These parrots sound like they are talking.

What They Look Like

Parrots can be many shapes and sizes. The pygmy parrot is only about four inches (10 cm) long. The hyacinth macaw can grow over three feet (one m) long.

Parrots are famous for their bright colors. Some parrots have red, blue, green, orange, or yellow feathers. Parrots can be white all over, too.

These colorful macaws are preening.

Parrots have thick, hooked beaks.
Parrots use their beaks to **preen**, dig,
and crack open nuts.

Climbing Birds

Parrots have good feet for climbing. Parrots have four toes on each foot. Two toes point forward and two toes point backward. A parrot can grip a tree branch tightly with its feet. Using their feet and strong beaks, parrots can climb trees. Parrots may be the best climbers of all birds.

Parrots are good at climbing.

Eating And Nesting

Parrots have a special way of eating. First, they grab food with their feet. Then, they lift the food to their mouths. Parrots mostly eat fruits, nuts, flowers, and seeds. They will eat insects and worms, too.

This blue-and-yellow macaw is eating a nut.

Many parrots nest in holes in trees. A parrot often shares its nest with a mate. Some parrots, like lovebirds, keep their mates for life.

African Gray Parrots

African gray parrots are among the smartest and best-known parrots. This parrot gets its name from its ash-gray feathers.

African gray parrots are some of the best "talking" parrots. They can **mimic** more than 100 different words. Many people keep African gray parrots as pets. As pets, these parrots may live longer than 60 years.

An African gray parrot.

Macaws

There are 16 **species** of macaws. The hyacinth macaw is the longest of all parrots. The blue-and-yellow macaw is a common macaw of South America.

Macaws are "talking" parrots, too. These colorful birds scream loudly and can bite very hard. Yet, many people have them as pets. As pets, macaws may live to be 70 years old.

A hyacinth macaw (right) with another colorful parrot.

Kakapos

The kakapo is one of the rarest birds. Some people call it the "owl parrot" of New Zealand. Like most owls, the kakapo comes out at night.

The kakapo has short wings. It is the only parrot that cannot fly. The kakapo is also the heaviest parrot. Some kakapos weigh as much as eight pounds (four kg).

A kakapo in its ground nest.

Parrot Chicks

A mother parrot commonly lays three, four, or five eggs. Parrot eggs are white, rough, and chalky. The parrot parents sit on their eggs until they hatch.

Baby parrots are called chicks. Newly hatched parrot chicks are featherless. Over many weeks, the chicks grow soft, down feathers. At eight weeks old, some parrots can already fly.

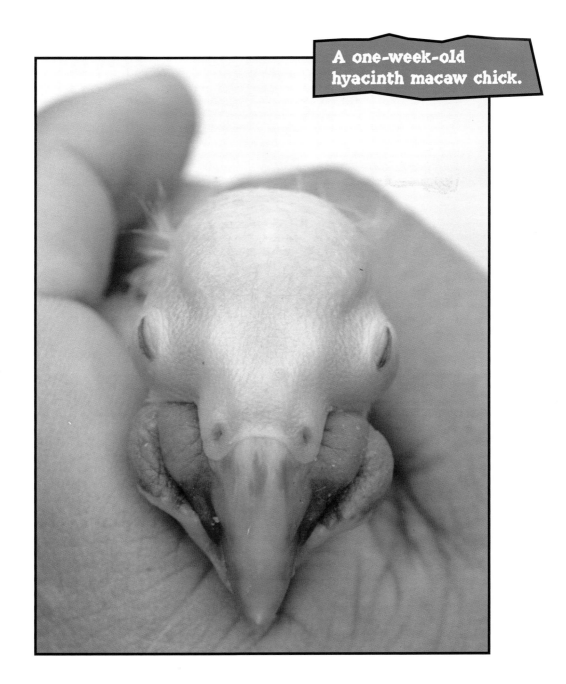

Parrots At Risk

Some species of parrots have died out. They are now extinct. About 90 species of parrots are at risk of becoming extinct. Two of these parrots are the hyacinth macaw and Spix's macaw.

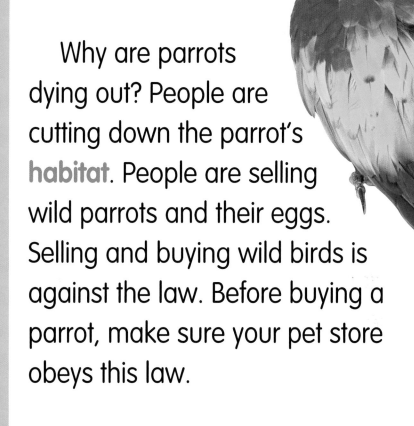

Why are parrots dying out? People are cutting down the parrot's **habitat**. People are selling wild parrots and their eggs. Selling and buying wild birds is against the law. Before buying a parrot, make sure your pet store obeys this law.

Important Words

extinct when all members of a species no longer exist, or live.

habitat where an animal lives in the wild.

mimic to copy what you see or hear. Some parrots can mimic sounds very well.

preen what birds do to clean themselves.

species living things that are very much alike.

Web Sites

Birdstation

www.petstation.com/birds.html#TOP
What would it be like to have a pet bird? Find
out here.

Those Majestic Macaws

www.exoticbird.com
Learn more about macaws at this web site.

The Tropics

http://tropics.parrotrefuge.com/index1.html
Visit this bird refuge and meet the exotic birds
that live there.

Index

Africa **4**

African gray parrot **12, 13**

Asia **4**

Australia **4**

beak **7, 8, 11**

blue-and-yellow
    macaw **11, 14**

Central America **4**

chicks **18, 19**

cockatoos **4**

extinct **20**

habitat **4, 21**

hyacinth macaw **6, 14, 15,
    19, 20**

kakapo **16, 17**

lovebirds **4, 11**

macaws **4, 6, 7, 11, 14, 15,
    19, 20**

mate **11**

mimic **5, 12**

nest **11, 16, 17**

New Zealand **16**

parakeets **4**

pygmy parrot **6**

South America **4, 14**

Spix's macaw **20**

toes **8**